TEAM TIME MACHINE: THE NEW NATION
TEAM TIME MACHINE
PICKS A PRESIDENT IN THE ELECTION OF 1800
I0821911
BY ELIZABETH KRAJNIK
Gareth Stevens
PUBLISHING

Please visit our website, www.garethstevens.com. For a free color catalog of all our high-quality books, call toll free 1-800-542-2595 or fax 1-877-542-2596.

Cataloging-in-Publication Data

Names: Krajnik, Elizabeth.
Title: Team time machine picks a president in the election of 1800 / Elizabeth Krajnik.
Description: New York : Gareth Stevens Publishing, 2021. | Series: Team time machine: the new nation | Includes glossary and index.
Identifiers: ISBN 9781538257036 (pbk.) | ISBN 9781538257050 (library bound) | ISBN 9781538257043 (6 pack)
Subjects: LCSH: Presidents–United States–Election–1800–Juvenile literature. | Elections–United States–Juvenile literature. | United States–Politics and government–1797-1801–Juvenile literature. | Political campaigns–United States–Juvenile literature.
Classification: LCC JK524.K73 2021 | DDC 324.60973–dc23

First Edition

Published in 2021 by
Gareth Stevens Publishing
111 East 14th Street, Suite 349
New York, NY 10003

Designer: Katelyn E. Reynolds
Editor: Therese Shea

Photo credits: Cover, p. 1 (both) courtesy of the Library of Congress; cover, pp. 1–24 (series characters) Lorelyn Medina/ Shutterstock.com; cover, pp. 1–24 (time machine elements) Agor2012/Shutterstock.com; cover, pp. 1–24 (background texture) somen/Shutterstock.com; p. 5 FG Trade/E+/Getty Images; p. 7 Thiranun Kunatum/Shutterstock.com; p. 9 (main) PAUL J.RICHARDS/AFP via Getty Images; p. 9 (inset) John Parrot/Stocktrek Images/Getty Images; p. 11 Lee Boltin/The LIFE Images Collection via Getty Images/Getty Images; p. 13 (main) New-York Historical Society/ Janneman/Wikipedia.org; p. 13 (inset) wynnter/ iStock / Getty Images Plus; p. 15 (Adams and Jefferson) THEPALMER/ DigitalVision Vectors/Getty Images; p. 15 (Pinckney) Kean Collection/Getty Images; p. 15 (Burr) Nawrocki/ClassicStock/Getty Images; p. 17 Tasoph/ Shutterstock.com; p. 21 Francis G. Mayer/Corbis/VCG via Getty Images; p. 23 GeorgiosArt/ iStock / Getty Images Plus; p. 25 National Arcives of the United States/NARA/ Keeleysam/Wikipedia.org; p. 27 GraphicaArtis/Getty Images; p. 29 The National Archives and Records Administration.

Printed in the United States of America

CONTENTS

WORDS IN THE GLOSSARY APPEAR IN **BOLD** TYPE THE FIRST TIME THEY ARE USED IN THE TEXT.

CHAPTER 1: THE TIEBREAKER

"I'm the winner!" Gaby yelled.

"No, I'm the winner!" Zoe shouted back.

The girls were on the swings. Each was trying to swing the highest.

"I can't tell," Will said as he looked up at them. "You need to do a tiebreaker."

"That reminds me of our reading for class today," Gaby said, putting her feet on the ground.

"Do you mean the tiebreaker for the election of 1800?" Will asked.

"What are you talking about?" Zoe asked. "I fell asleep reading last night."

MEET TEAM TIME MACHINE

TEAM TIME MACHINE IS A GROUP OF FRIENDS WHO FOUND A TIME MACHINE ONE DAY IN A VERY ODD LIBRARY. THEY DISCOVERED THAT BOOKS FROM THE LIBRARY COULD POWER THE MACHINE AND TRANSPORT THEM TO DIFFERENT PLACES AND TIMES. IN THIS ADVENTURE, GABY, ZOE, AND WILL LEARN ABOUT THE ELECTION OF 1800!

A TIEBREAKER IS A CONTEST USED TO SELECT A WINNER WHEN ANOTHER CONTEST ENDS IN A TIE. THE ELECTION OF 1800 NEEDED A TIEBREAKER!

"Two **candidates** received the same number of votes during the presidential election of 1800," Gaby explained to Zoe. "The House of Representatives had to decide the winner."

"Let's go to the library and show Zoe what happened," Will said with a smile.

Once they got to the library, Gaby asked, "Zoe, can you grab the book called *The Election of 1800*?"

As soon as Zoe placed the book in the machine and pulled the handle, they journeyed back in time!

TEAM TIME MACHINE CAN GO TO ANY TIME AND ANY PLACE. ALL THEY HAVE TO DO IS FIND A BOOK ABOUT IT ON THE SHELF, PLACE IT IN A SLOT IN THE TIME MACHINE, AND PULL THE HANDLE.

CHAPTER 2: RIVAL CAMPAIGNS

The team stepped out of the library into the new capital city of the young United States—Washington, DC! They heard someone shouting and decided to see what was going on. They walked to a town park and saw a man yelling about the Federalist Party.

Will explained, "The Federalist Party is the party John Adams belonged to. It was one of the first two American **political parties**. The other party is the Democratic-Republican Party, which Thomas Jefferson belonged to. Adams and Jefferson were the two main presidential candidates in 1800."

PRESIDENTIAL CANDIDATES DIDN'T **CAMPAIGN** LIKE THEY DO TODAY. THIS JOB WAS GIVEN TO OTHERS IN A CANDIDATE'S POLITICAL PARTY. THEY SPOKE OUT IN FAVOR OF THEIR CANDIDATE.

MONTICELLO WAS THOMAS JEFFERSON'S HOME. HE STAYED THERE FROM MAY TO NOVEMBER IN 1800 WHILE OTHERS CAMPAIGNED FOR HIM.

THOMAS JEFFERSON

The man in the park shouted, "Adams and the Federalists will ruin our **democratic** government! We need Jefferson!"

"Why is that guy so upset?" Zoe asked.

Gaby said, "In 1800, John Adams ran for reelection as a Federalist. Thomas Jefferson and other Democratic-Republicans disagreed with the Federalists' ideas. They worried the national government was becoming too powerful. They thought the states and people were losing rights."

Will added, "At the same time, the Federalists said Jefferson would throw the country into **chaos** if *he* became president!"

EVEN PEOPLE WITHIN THE FEDERALIST PARTY DISAGREED WITH SOME OF ADAMS' CHOICES DURING HIS PRESIDENCY. THESE PEOPLE WERE KNOWN AS ULTRAS.

DURING ADAMS' PRESIDENCY, HE HELPED MAKE PEACE WITH FRANCE. THIS CAUSED THE ULTRAS TO BREAK AWAY FROM THE FEDERALISTS.
JOHN ADAMS

CHAPTER 3: THE CANDIDATES

"Wow," said Zoe. "I guess people have always fought about **politics**!"

"And, back then, people who wanted to be president and vice president all ran on the same **ballot**," Will said. "Whoever got the most votes became president and whoever got the second most votes became vice president."

Gaby chimed in, "In 1800, the Democratic-Republican Party chose Jefferson as their first choice and Aaron Burr as the other candidate. The Federalist Party chose John Adams and Charles Cotesworth Pinckney to run."

THE WAY THE BALLOT WORKED IN THE EARLY DAYS OF THE UNITED STATES MEANT THAT PEOPLE OF DIFFERENT POLITICAL PARTIES COULD BE ELECTED PRESIDENT AND VICE PRESIDENT.

AARON BURR WAS 44 WHEN HE WAS CHOSEN AS A CANDIDATE FOR THE 1800 ELECTION. HE WAS SERVING AS A MEMBER OF THE NEW YORK LEGISLATURE, THE STATE'S LAWMAKING BODY.

AARON BURR

CHARLES COTESWORTH PINCKNEY

"But what if the president and vice president who are elected have different points of view on an issue?" Zoe asked.

"Exactly! Most of the time, parties chose two candidates to run together on the ballot, just like Aaron Burr and Thomas Jefferson," Will said. "They hoped that their candidates would win president and vice president, but there was no way to make sure."

"In our time, candidates for president and vice president are chosen as a team by the Electoral College," Will said.

RESULTS OF THE ELECTION OF 1796

JOHN ADAMS

POLITICAL PARTY:
FEDERALIST

ELECTORAL VOTES:
71

THOMAS JEFFERSON

POLITICAL PARTY:
DEMOCRATIC-REPUBLICAN

ELECTORAL VOTES:
68

THOMAS PINCKNEY

POLITICAL PARTY:
FEDERALIST

ELECTORAL VOTES:
59

AARON BURR

POLITICAL PARTY:
DEMOCRATIC-REPUBLICAN

ELECTORAL VOTES:
30

IN THE ELECTION OF 1796, JOHN ADAMS WAS ELECTED PRESIDENT AND THOMAS JEFFERSON WAS ELECTED VICE PRESIDENT. THESE MEN BELONGED TO OPPOSING POLITICAL PARTIES.

CHAPTER 4: CASTING AND COUNTING VOTES

"Didn't the time machine say this is February 11, 1801?" asked Zoe. "Wasn't the U.S. election in 1800? Did we travel too far?"

"Well," Gaby replied, "the votes weren't counted until February 11."

"Right, the votes were cast in each state capital in December 1800," said Will. "They were sent to Washington, DC, to be counted. But nearly everyone knew the results before the official count."

"So? Don't keep me waiting!" said Zoe excitedly. "What happened?"

"Let's go see!" said Gaby.

The kids walked to the **Capitol** to watch the counting of the votes.

BACK THEN, ELECTORS IN THE ELECTORAL COLLEGE WERE CHOSEN BY STATE LEGISLATURES. IN OUR TIME, WE ELECT THE ELECTORS THROUGH THE **POPULAR VOTE**.

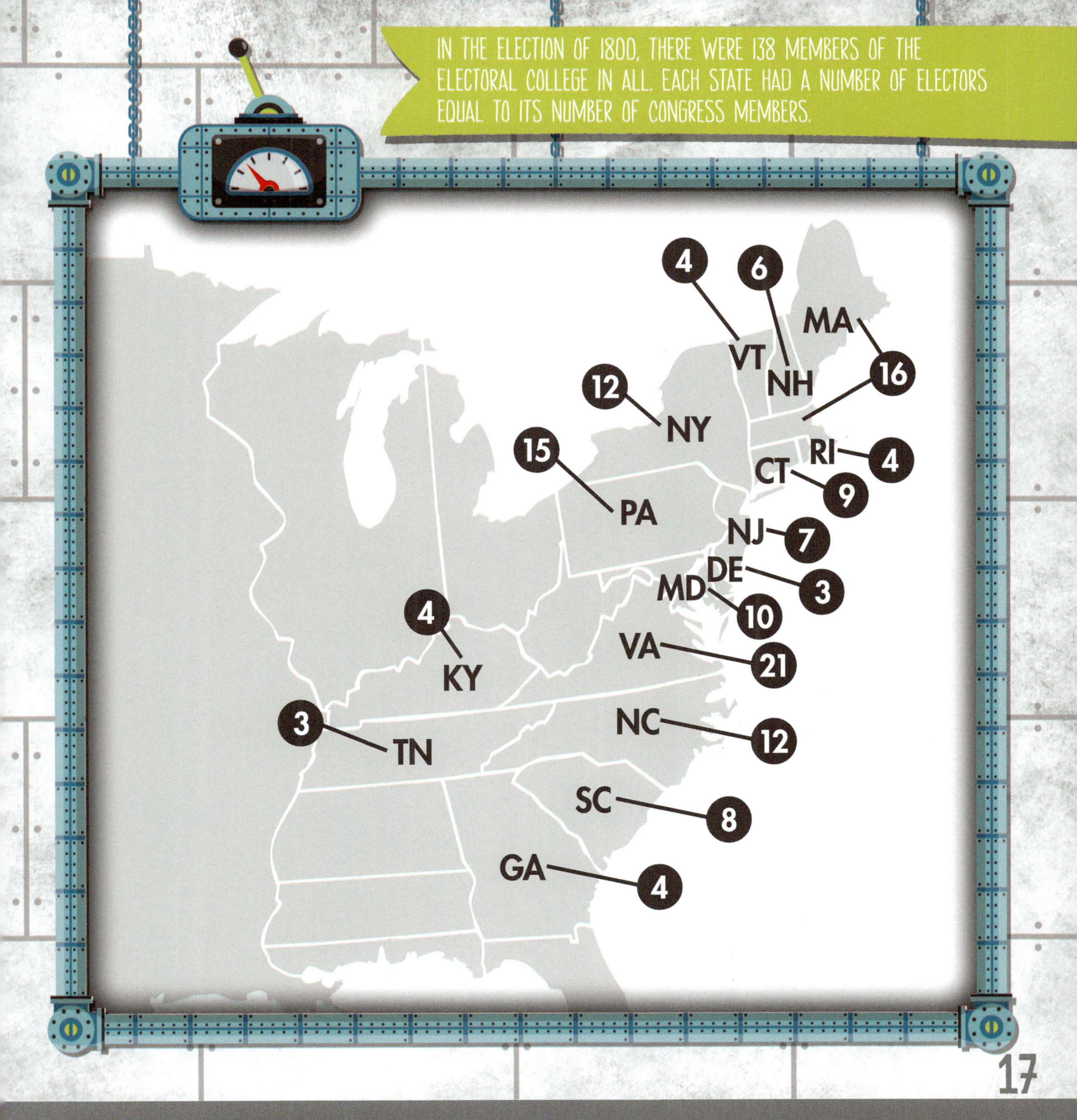
IN THE ELECTION OF 1800, THERE WERE 138 MEMBERS OF THE ELECTORAL COLLEGE IN ALL. EACH STATE HAD A NUMBER OF ELECTORS EQUAL TO ITS NUMBER OF CONGRESS MEMBERS.
VT 4
NH 6
MA 16
NY 12
RI 4
PA 15
CT 9
NJ 7
DE 3
MD 10
KY 4
VA 21
TN 3
NC 12
SC 8
GA 4

All the members of the House of Representatives and the Senate were gathered in the Capitol. Since Thomas Jefferson was vice president, he led the Senate. He called out the votes. The kids listened at the back of the chamber, or room. It became clear John Adams wasn't going to win.

"The Democratic-Republicans are headed to the White House," Gaby said.

"But who will be president?" asked Zoe. "Thomas Jefferson or Aaron Burr?"

Will laughed, "If you had done the reading, you'd know Jefferson and Burr tie!"

THE ELECTION RESULTS WEREN'T SUPPOSED TO BE OPENED UNTIL FEBRUARY 11, 1801. HOWEVER, THE RESULTS WERE LEAKED JUST NINE DAYS AFTER THEY WERE CAST ON DECEMBER 3.

STATE	JEFFERSON	BURR	ADAMS	PINCKNEY	JAY
CONNECTICUT			9	9	
DELAWARE			3	3	
GEORGIA	4	4			
KENTUCKY	4	4			
MARYLAND	5	5	5	5	
MASSACHUSETTS			16	16	
NEW HAMPSHIRE			6	6	
NEW JERSEY			7	7	
NEW YORK	12	12			
NORTH CAROLINA	8	8	4	4	
PENNSYLVANIA	8	8	7	7	
RHODE ISLAND			4	3	1
SOUTH CAROLINA	8	8			
TENNESSEE	3	3			
VERMONT			4	4	
VIRGINIA	21	21			
TOTAL	73	73	65	64	1

The House chamber was humming with excitement about the election results.

"Wow, a tie!" Zoe exclaimed. "How will they choose the next president then?"

Just then, a congressman made an announcement: "The nation's highest law, the Constitution, has an answer for our problem. It says said that if two presidential candidates tie, each state in the House of Representatives shall cast one vote to decide the winner."

"Let's stay for the vote," Zoe said to her friends.

WE DIDN'T GET TO VOTE,
BUT WE TOLD A FEW CONGRESSMEN IN
THE HOUSE OF REPRESENTATIVES
OUR OPINION! WE PICKED JEFFERSON
FOR PRESIDENT.

MANY FEDERALISTS DIDN'T LIKE THOMAS JEFFERSON. THEY WERE PREPARED TO VOTE FOR AARON BURR. HOWEVER, FEDERALIST ALEXANDER HAMILTON AND BURR WERE ENEMIES. HAMILTON CAMPAIGNED AGAINST BURR.

CHAPTER 6: THE FINAL VOTE

Team Time Machine spent six days at the Capitol. The winner of the election needed a **majority** of the votes. On February 17, 1801, the House of Representatives voted for the thirty-sixth time! Thomas Jefferson finally received the number of votes he needed to defeat Aaron Burr.

"I'm so glad they decided," Zoe sighed. "What made the voters change their minds?"

Will whispered, "I heard James Bayard of Delaware agreed to cast a blank vote if Jefferson promised to work with the Federalists. That gave Jefferson a majority."

SOME PEOPLE WORRIED THAT AMERICANS WOULD BEGIN FIGHTING IF AARON BURR WAS ELECTED.

JAMES BAYARD WAS A FEDERALIST FROM DELAWARE. HE DECIDED JEFFERSON WAS A BETTER CHOICE THAN BURR.

CHAPTER 7: A CHANGE TO THE CONSTITUTION

As the team left the Capitol, Zoe asked, "Was there ever another tie like this in the presidential election?"

"The Twelfth **Amendment** to the Constitution changed how elections worked," Will replied. "Instead of electors casting two votes for president, they chose a president and a vice president. If a tie happens, the House of Representatives votes for one of the top three candidates."

Gaby said, "Political parties also began choosing presidential and vice presidential candidates to run together."

IT'S IMPORTANT TO VOTE IN AN ELECTION IF YOU CAN. YOUR VOTE HELPS CHOOSE WHICH ELECTORS WILL VOTE FOR THE PRESIDENT AND VICE PRESIDENT.

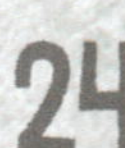

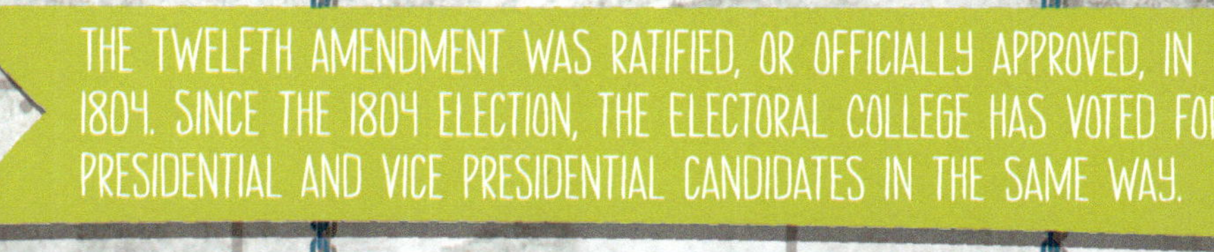

THE TWELFTH AMENDMENT WAS RATIFIED, OR OFFICIALLY APPROVED, IN 1804. SINCE THE 1804 ELECTION, THE ELECTORAL COLLEGE HAS VOTED FOR PRESIDENTIAL AND VICE PRESIDENTIAL CANDIDATES IN THE SAME WAY.

CONGRESS OF THE UNITED STATES;

AT THE FIRST SESSION,

Begun and held at the city of Washington, in the territory of Columbia, on Monday, the seventeenth of October, one thousand eight hundred and three.

Resolved by the **Senate** and **House** of **Representatives** of the *United States* of *America*, in Congress assembled,

Two thirds of both houses concurring, that in lieu of the third paragraph of the first section of the second article of the constitution of the United States, the following be proposed as an amendment to the constitution of the United States, which when ratified by three fourths of the legislatures of the several states, shall be valid to all intents and purposes, as part of the said constitution, to wit:

The Electors shall meet in their respective states, and vote by ballot for President and Vice-President, one of whom, at least, shall not be an inhabitant of the same state with themselves; they shall name in their ballots the person voted for as President, and in distinct ballots the person voted for as Vice President, and they shall make distinct lists of all persons voted for as President, and of all persons voted for as Vice President, and of the number of votes for each, which lists they shall sign and certify, and transmit sealed to the seat of the government of the United States, directed to the President of the Senate; The President of the Senate shall, in the presence of the Senate and House of Representatives, open all the certificates and the votes shall then be counted; The person having the greatest number of votes for President, shall be the President, if such number be a majority of the whole number of Electors appointed; and if no person have such majority, then from the persons having the highest numbers not exceeding three on the list of those voted for as President, the House of Representatives shall choose immediately, by ballot, the President. But in choosing the President, the votes shall be taken by states, the representation from each state having one vote; a quorum for this purpose shall consist of a member or members from two thirds of the states, and a majority of all the states shall be necessary to a choice. And if the House of Representatives shall not choose a President whenever the right of choice shall devolve upon them, before the fourth day of March next following, then the Vice President shall act as President, as in the case of the death or other constitutional disability of the President. The person having the greatest number of votes as Vice President, shall be the Vice President, if such number be a majority of the whole number of Electors appointed, and if no person have a majority, then from the two highest numbers on the list, the Senate shall choose the Vice President;

CHAPTER 8: BACK TO THE PRESENT

"I'm glad it's over," Zoe said as they walked back to their library.

Will yawned, "We haven't gotten much sleep since the voting started!"

"I'm ready to go back to our time—and take a nap. What about you?" Gaby asked.

"Yes! Let's fire up the time machine," Zoe said happily.

Will took the book out of the time machine and put it back on the shelf. The room began to shake as the team was transported back to school in their own time.

AFTER THOMAS JEFFERSON BECAME PRESIDENT, HE TRIED TO BRING TOGETHER PEOPLE OF DIFFERENT POLITICAL PARTIES. HE SAID PEOPLE COULD HAVE DIFFERENT IDEAS AND STILL GET ALONG.

THOMAS JEFFERSON'S **INAUGURATION** TOOK PLACE ON MARCH 4, 1801. WASHINGTON AND ADAMS HAD WORN SPECIAL SUITS AND RODE IN CARRIAGES TO THEIR INAUGURATIONS. JEFFERSON WORE PLAIN CLOTHES AND WALKED TO THE CAPITOL.

When Zoe, Gaby, and Will got back to school, they sat down at a table.

Zoe said, "I don't think I'll do the reading for class today. I learned so much, thanks to the time machine."

"I think you should still do the reading," Gaby replied. "After all, we didn't get to see the whole election, just the vote in the House of Representatives."

"I agree with Gaby," Will said. "So I'm the tiebreaker! It's two against one!"

"Okay, okay!" laughed Zoe. "I'd better start reading!"

A HISTORIC ELECTION

DECEMBER 3, 1800 — ELECTORS IN THE ELECTORAL COLLEGE CAST THEIR VOTES FOR PRESIDENT. THOMAS JEFFERSON AND AARON BURR RECEIVE THE SAME NUMBER OF VOTES.

FEBRUARY 11, 1801 — THE HOUSE OF REPRESENTATIVES BEGINS TO CAST THEIR VOTES. NEITHER BURR NOR JEFFERSON RECEIVE A MAJORITY AT FIRST.

FEBRUARY 17, 1801 — THE HOUSE OF REPRESENTATIVES CASTS ITS THIRTY-SIXTH VOTE. THOMAS JEFFERSON WINS THE ELECTION.

MARCH 4, 1801 — THOMAS JEFFERSON IS INAUGURATED THE THIRD PRESIDENT OF THE UNITED STATES.

JUNE 15, 1804 — THE TWELFTH AMENDMENT TO THE U.S. CONSTITUTION IS RATIFIED, CHANGING HOW U.S. ELECTIONS WORK.

	Thomas Jefferson of Virginia	Aaron Burr of New York	John Adams of Massachusetts	Charles C. Pinckney of South Carolina	John Jay of New York
New Hampshire			6	6	
Massachusetts			16	16	
Rhode Island			4	3	1
Connecticut			9	9	
Vermont			4	4	
New York	12	12			
New Jersey			7	7	
Pennsylvania	8	8	7	7	
Delaware			3	3	
Maryland	5	5	5	5	
Virginia	21	21			
Kentucky	4	4			
North Carolina	8	8	4	4	
Tennessee	3	3			
South Carolina	8	8			
Georgia	4	4			
	73	73	65	64	1

THIS IS THE RECORD OF THE ELECTORS' VOTES FROM THE 1800 PRESIDENTIAL ELECTION.

GLOSSARY

amendment: a change or addition to a constitution

ballot: a sheet of paper listing candidates' names and used for voting

campaign: a series of activities designed to produce a particular result

candidate: a person who is trying to be elected

Capitol: the building where U.S. Congress meets in Washington, DC

chaos: total confusion and disorder

democratic: describing a form of government in which all citizens participate

inauguration: a ceremony marking the start of someone's term in public office

majority: a number that is greater than half of a total

political party: a group of people with similar beliefs and ideas about government who work to have their members elected to government positions

politics: the activities of the government and government officials

popular vote: the votes of all people in a country, rather than the votes of a group such as the Electoral College

FOR MORE INFORMATION

BOOKS

Oachs, Emily Rose. *Thomas Jefferson's Presidency.* Minneapolis, MN: Lerner Publications, 2017.

Worth, Richard. *Alexander Hamilton and Aaron Burr.* New York, NY: Enslow, 2018.

WEBSITES

Campaign of 1800
www.pbs.org/video/first-freedom-campaign-1800/
Watch a video about this history-making election.

The Election of 1800
www.socialstudiesforkids.com/articles/ushistory/electionof1800.htm
Read about the influence of Alexander Hamilton on the election.

The Election of 1800
www.ushistory.org/us/20a.asp
Need more historical facts? Find them here.

Publisher's note to educators and parents: Our editors have carefully reviewed these websites to ensure that they are suitable for students. Many websites change frequently, however, and we cannot guarantee that a site's future contents will continue to meet our high standards of quality and educational value. Be advised that students should be closely supervised whenever they access the internet.

INDEX